All Righ

This book or any portion thereo
any manner whatsoever withou.
the publisher except for the use of brief quotations in a book review.

Disclaimer

The information provided herein is stated to be truthful and consistent, in that any liability, in terms of inattention or otherwise, by any usage or abuse of any policies, processes, or directions contained within is the solitary and utter responsibility of the recipient reader.

The information herein is offered for informational purposes solely, and is universal as so. The presentation of the information is without contract or any type of guarantee assurance.

Under no circumstances will any legal responsibility or blame be held against the author or publisher for any reparation, damages, or monetary loss due to the information herein, either directly or indirectly.

Before Getting Started

First and foremost thank you for downloading my cookbook. Many well-established kitchen gurus have helped with crafting these unique recipes and without their contributions this would not be possible. I sincerely hope you enjoy it.

Also, if you would be kind enough to leave a positive review on Amazon it would be greatly appreciated. You have no idea how much it helps us independent authors!

Your friend,
Carla

Table of Contents

Teriyaki Glazed Halibut Steak	9
Air Fried Sweet Potato Pie	10
Stuffed Mushrooms	12
Crumbed Chicken Tenderloins, Fried in Thin Air	13
Jerk Chicken Wings	14
Crumbed Potato Balls	16
Bacon Wrapped Prawns	18
Pizza for One – Crustless	19
Chocolate Cake in an Air Fryer	20
Coconut Pie	21
Peanut Fluff Samosas	23
Good Butter Best Cake	25
Rosemary Chips	26
Classic Grilled Cheese for Two (or One)	27
Parmesan Schnitzel for One	28
Roast Lamb Chops	29
Ba–corn Crustless Quiche	31
Chimichurri Skirt Steak	33
Buttermilk Biscuits	34
Air Fried Pecan Pie	36
Stuffed Pumpkin	38
Stuffed Potatoes	39
Cajun Shrimp with Jambalaya Rice	41
Air Fried Broccoli	43
Chicken Fillets, Brie & Ham	44
Beef & Lemon Schnitzel for One	45
Donuts & Cinnamon	46

Tasty Tenders	48
Korean Chicken Satay	49
Steamed Salmon & Sauce	50
Onion Flowers	51
Pork & Peanut Satay	52
Tossed Vegetable Medley	54
Stuffed Peppers	55
Radish & Mozzarella Salad	56
Marinated Cornish Hen	57
Air Fried Banana Bread	58
Cheesy Garlic Bread	60
Flying Fish	61
French Air Fried Beans	62
Shirred Eggs	63
Simple Spring Rolls	65
Baked Tomato & Feta	67
Crisp Crunch Crab Cakes	69
Sweet Potato Chips	71
Air Fried Mac & Cheese Wheel	72
Hamionshroom Quiche	74
Vanilla Soufflé	76
Crispy Nachos Prawns	78
Curried Cauliflower Florets	79

Introduction

What is an Air Fryer?

"What's all the fuss?" you may ask, "Do we suddenly all neeeeed air fryers in our lives?" The short and sweet answer is: you don't.

However, if you find yourself sneaking through the drive thru in the hopes that your more logical self will not notice, you may wish to read further. Firstly, because you can make fries at home while in your pajamas, secondly, it uses far less oil (think 70% or so less) and, thirdly, you will be pecking away at your meal quicker than the wait time at the collection window. After your initial investment, the machine will begin to pay itself off in no time.

A renowned chef who has something blunt and honest to say about most things he encounters, including the dubious concept of frying chips in thin air, noted that nothing can replace the flavor of deep frying.

He pointed out that potatoes and 1 tablespoon of oil yield a great-tasting and way healthier result. Air fried chips are tender on the inside, and beautifully crisp on the outside. The conclusion then: *we* need to redefine our definition of how "real" chips "should" taste.

This may be a hard concept to swallow without a large soda, but it by no means negates the point of said gadget. If you don't fancy baked potatoes masquerading as their densely polyunsaturated relatives, think of chocolate cake instead. Yep, that's right.

History Behind the Air Fryer

Step aside Microwave, you have been surpassed by a young whipper-snapper named The Mighty Air Fryer, who hopped onto the shelves in the appliance section circa 2010.

Health nuts were responsible for their release in Australia and Europe. America and Japan joined in the fun shortly afterward. Australian and European health nuts released them first, and then in!

Tips for Cooking with an Air Fryer

How hard is it to use these new-fangled appliances? Not very. There is a timer, an on-off switch, and a temperature dial. Fancier models have all kinds of extra bells and whistles, but you are welcome to ignore them. All you need to understand is that it works by fanning heat around your food. Add a bit of water and basic steaming becomes possible!

Many recipes call for you to preheat the fryer. Besides being an absolutely illogical concept (an oven has two states: heated or unheated), this step is up to you. Bigger ovens function best when they are rearing to go, especially halogen ovens (the big brother of the air fryer). But wait, there's more!

If you live alone, this is a vital addition to your kitchen because it is compact and doesn't use a ton of energy. If you are always in a hurry, consider buying one immediately. If you have a family, get a bigger one (fryer, that is) so you don't spend your time on this earth stuck in the kitchen at the bidding of tiny humans. If you are a health nut, you have no choice but to buy one.

So, maybe you might jusssst need one after all. Before you rush off to the store, though, do your homework to ensure you get a fryer that suits your needs.

Fry responsibly.

Recipes

Teriyaki Glazed Halibut Steak

Serve with white rice & mint chutney

Serves: 2
Time to Prepare: 30 min

Ingredients

- 1 lb Halibut Steak
- ⅔ cup Soy Sauce
- ½ cup Dry Sherry (or Mirin, if you want to be authentic)
- ¼ cup Table Sugar
- 1 Lime, Juiced (2 Tbsp)
- 1 Small Orange, Juiced (¼ cup)
- ¼ Tsp Red Pepper Flakes, Crushed
- ¼ Tsp Ground Ginger
- 1 Crushed Clove of Garlic

Directions

Gently boil all the ingredients together in a pot (except the halibut) until reduced by half.

Once cooled a bit, pour into a zip-seal bag with the fish & refrigerate for ±30 minutes.

Preheat (if needed) the fryer to 390° F so long & once the fish is ready, remove it from the pouch & cook for ±10 min.

Brush with a bit of the marinade when you take it out the fryer.

Air Fried Sweet Potato Pie

Here's something different to add to your repertoire. Super easy & you can even use leftover sweet potato from the night before to make this pie!

Serves: 2
Time to Prepare: 10 min

Ingredients

- 1 x 6 oz Sweet Potato
- 1 Tsp Vegetable Oil
- 1 x 9" Rolled out Pie Dough at Room Temperature
- 3 Medium Eggs
- ¼ cup Heavy Cream
- 2 Tbsp Maple Syrup
- 1 Tbsp Brown Sugar
- 1 Tbsp Butter (Melted)
- ¾ Tsp Vanilla Essence/Extract
- ½ Tsp Salt
- ½ Tsp Cinnamon
- A Generous Pinch of Nutmeg (⅛ Tsp)

Directions

Cook the sweet potato (in its skin) in the fryer first: coat it with oil & set the temp to 400° F for 30 min. It should be nice & tender. Cool for 20 min or so, then peel & mash. Set one side.

Meanwhile, prepare the pie shell. Lay it out onto a lightly floured work surface & use an 8" pie plate as a template to cut around with a knife.

Grease the pie pan & carefully lay the dough into it. Fold the edges under themselves & squish them with a fork or something to make them look pretty. Cover & set aside.

Whisk together the eggs, cream, syrup, sugar, butter, vanilla, salt, cinnamon, & nutmeg. Fold in the mash & pour into the pie shell. Cook at 320° F until the pie is set & the crust is just perfect (30 min)

Leave the pie to cool for 20 min before slicing & serving.

Serve with whipped cream… yum.

Stuffed Mushrooms

Mushrooms with a sour cream filling topped with cheese & fried... yummy

Serves: 12
Time to Prepare: 15 min

Ingredients

- 2 Rashers Bacon, Diced
- ½ Onion, Diced
- ½ Bell Pepper, Diced
- 1 Small Carrot, Diced
- 24 Medium Size Mushrooms (Separate the caps & stalks)
- 1 cup Shredded Cheddar Plus Extra for the Top
- ½ cup Sour Cream

Directions

Chop the mushrooms stalks finely & fry them up with the bacon, onion, pepper & carrot.

When the veggies are fairly tender, stir in the sour cream & the cheese. Keep on the heat until the cheese has melted & everything is mixed nicely.

Now grab the mushroom caps & heap a plop of filling on each one. Place in the fryer basket & top with a little extra cheese.

Cook at 350° F for 8 min.

Crumbed Chicken Tenderloins, Fried in Thin Air

This will most likely be preferred by the family to fast-food chicken

Serves: 4
Time to Prepare: 10 min

Ingredients

- 2 Tbsp Vegetable Oil, or Butter
- 1.75 oz Breadcrumbs
- 1 Egg, Whisked
- 8 Chicken Tenderloins

Directions

Mix the oil & breadcrumbs together until most of the oil has been absorbed & the mix is crumbly, place in a soup plate.

Next, put the whisked egg in a soup plate.

First, dip the chicken in the egg, shake off any big drips, coat with crumbs & carefully lay in the fryer basket. Cook at 350° F for 12 min.

If you have very big pieces, cook for a little longer. Tada!

Jerk Chicken Wings

This is easier than it looks. Check the one-step directions. Ok, maybe 2 or 3 steps. Chop everything really fine. Let it rest. Then cook it!

Serves: 6
Time to Prepare: 15 min

Ingredients

- 4 lb Wings (Chicken that is)
- 2 Tbsp Oil
- 2 Tbsp Soy Sauce
- 6 Finely Minced Cloves of Garlic
- 1 Habanero Chili, Cleaned Up & Minced
- 1 Tbsp Allspice (Note: This is not the same as mixed spice)
- 1 Tsp Cinnamon
- 1 Tsp Cayenne Pepper
- 1 Tsp White Pepper (Less overpowering than black pepper)
- 1 Tbsp Freshly Minced Thyme
- 2 Tbsp Sticky Brown Sugar
- 1 Small Grated Ginger Root (1 Tbsp)
- 4 Finely Chopped Green Onions
- 2-3 Limes for Fresh Juice (5 Tbsp)
- ½ cup Wine Vinegar (Red is great)
- 1 Tsp Salt

Directions

Mix everything together in a large bowl & cover with cling film. Leave it in the fridge overnight if possible (2-24hrs).

Tip: if your fridge is full & cannot accommodate the bowl, scoop the mixture into a large zip-seal baggy instead.

If you need to preheat your fryer, do so now at 390° F.

Drain the wings of all liquid. Cook for ±15 min, half at a time to avoid over-crowding.

Give the basket a shake to ensure even cooking half-way through.

Crumbed Potato Balls

The air fryer version of the traditional potato croquette. Use a good quality mashing potato. Scale the recipe up if need be & cook in batches.

Serves: 2
Time to Prepare: 30 min

Ingredients

- 2 Peeled & Cubed, Med-sized Potatoes
- 1 Egg Yolk
- ½ cup Grated Parmesan
- 2 Tbsp Flour
- 2 Tbsp Freshly Chopped Chives
- Salt & Black Pepper to Taste
- A Pinch of Nutmeg
- 1½ Tbsp Olive Oil
- ½ cup Flour
- 1 Egg
- ½ cup Store-bought Breadcrumbs (Flavor to your discretion)

Directions

Bring a pot of salted water to the boil & cook the potatoes until tender (10-15 min). Mash them finely & set aside.

Mix the oil & the crumbs together until they are loose. Set aside.

Once the mash has cooled, mix in the yolk, cheese, flour, seasoning, chives & nutmeg. Make shapes from the resulting dough – either with cookie cutters or just roll into a simple ball.

Carefully dust each ball with flour so that you can handle it. Then dip in the egg & finally into the crumbs. Press the crumbs in gently.

If your fryer needs preheating, then get it up to 390° F so long. Pop the balls/shapes into the basket & cook until golden (7–8 min).

Bacon Wrapped Prawns

Well. Need we say more. It involves bacon; it's worth trying… Oh, & it's super easy & super tasty.

Serves: 4
Time to Prepare: 30 min

Ingredients

- 1 lb Tiger Prawns, Peeled & Deveined (± 4–5 Prawns Ea)
- 1 lb Bacon Strips at Room Temp

Directions

Grab a prawn & start winding the bacon strip around from the head down to the tail. Repeat… & put all the little parcels on a platter. Return them to the fridge for 20 min or so.

Make tea while you wait.

Preheat your fryer (if needed) to 390° F & cook them for ±6 minutes. Don't forget about your tea..

Pizza for One – Crustless

Perfect for gluten free diets or just for the love of mushrooms

Serves: 1
Time from Start to Finish: 5 min

Ingredients

- 1 x Enormous Portabella Mushroom Cap
- 1 Tbsp Olive Oil
- 1 Tbsp Canned Tomato & Basil Mix
- Mozzarella (As much as you would like)
- 4 Slices or So of Pepperoni
- A Pinch of Salt
- 1 Pinch Italian Herb Seasoning

Directions

Scoop the mushroom center out very carefully & drizzle the cap with olive oil (top & bottom sides).

Throw a bit of salt & seasoning around the interior before spooning some tomato into the cavity & top with cheese.

Carefully put it in the fryer basket & cook at 320° F (preheat if you like) ±5 min. But pop the pepperoni on after the first minute or so.

Finish it off with a bit of parmesan & crushed red pepper flakes.

Chocolate Cake in an Air Fryer

Hah! Who said an air fryer was only good for potatoes? This is simple, tasty & quick. A must-try recipe!

Serves: 2
Time to Prepare: 15 min

Ingredients

- 1.75 oz Fine Sugar
- 2 oz Butter (Slightly softened, but not melted)
- 1 Egg
- 1 Tbsp Apricot Jelly
- 1.75 oz White Cake Flour
- 1 Tbsp Unsweetened Cocoa Powder
- Salt, to Taste
- Confectioner's Sugar (Icing sugar) for Dusting

Directions

Spray a smallish cake ring with cooking spray.

Cream the sugar & butter together, then add the egg & apricot jelly. Sift in the dry ingredients & mix. Pour into the cake ring, put the ring in the fryer basket & cook at 320° F for 15 min.

Check to see if it is ready by pushing a skewer/knife/toothpick into the middle. If it comes out clean, you are good to go.

Leave to cool & dust with icing sugar.

Coconut Pie

This is a delicious coconut–custard prepared either in one 6" pan or in four little ramekins. Serve cold with toasted coconut & orange sauce.

Serves: 4
Time to Prepare: 20 min

Ingredients

- 2 cups Boiling Water

Caramel:

- ½ cup Plain Sugar & 1½ Tbsp Water
- ¾ cup Coconut Milk (Canned)
- ¼ cup Evaporated Milk
- ¼ cup Condensed Milk
- 2 Eggs
- 1 Egg Yolk
- ¼ cup Shredded (Toasted) Coconut
- A Little Orange Sauce for Serving

Directions

Heat to 320° F. Pour the two cups of boiling water into the fryer. Close the machine & leave to steam. Spray your ramekins or pan with cooking spray & set aside.

Now make the caramel by melting the sugar & water together over a medium heat. Keep the pan swirling & watch over it until it starts to turn a beautiful, well, caramel color (±10 min). Take off the heat immediately & pour into the pan or share between the ramekins.

Mix together the evaporated milk, condensed milk, & coconut milk & then whisk in the eggs & yolk.

Once this is all nicely blended, carefully ladle into the pan/ramekins. Pour in over the back of a tablespoon if you prefer.

Cover the pan/ramekins with foil & bake in the steamy air fryer at 320° F for 30 min.

Once done, remove the foil & set in the fridge for at least 2 hours to set. Scatter the toasted coconut over the top & serve with a little orange sauce.

Peanut Fluff Samosas

A delightful mix of peanuts & marshmallow fluff, all wrapped in a nice neat parcel. Try experimenting with other nut butters for a different spin on the same concept.

Serves: 4
Time to Prepare: 15 min

Ingredients

- 4 Sheets of Filo Pastry, Room Temp
- 4 Tbsp Crunchy Peanut Butter
- 4 Tsp Marshmallow Fluff
- 2 oz Butter
- A Pinch of Sea Salt – to Taste

Directions

Lay the four sheets of pastry one on top of the other with butter brushed between each layer. Now carefully slice 3x12" strips (should yield four).

Remove the top layer of pastry & spread one side with a Tbsp of peanut butter with a Tsp of fluff & return it to its pile. Now carefully take one corner & fold it over on itself to form a triangle. Fold it over itself again & continue like this all the way to the end of the strip. Use a little butter to seal the end.

Place into the fryer basket & cook until golden & fluffy (± 3–5 min @ 360° F). When they come out sprinkle a tiny pinch of sea salt over them.

This will give them that Junoesque that makes them feel more gourmet than kiddie's party. Not that kids can't eat gourmet food, or adults party food, but I'm sure you get the idea.

Note: If you are having difficulty keeping the filling in place while folding, feel free to experiment with other methods like, for example, using only two sheets instead. Just be mindful of sharing the peanut butter & fluff accordingly. Alternatively, just dump a blob of filling on the end & wrap the pastry around it. Whatever works best.

Good Butter Best Cake

Air fryers can bake a really good cake. Go ahead & give this one a try – it's dead easy.

Serves: 2
Time to Prepare: 15 min

Ingredients

- 3.5 oz Butter, Room Temperature
- 3 oz Fine Granulated Sugar (Castor)
- 1 Egg
- 7 oz White Cake Flour
- A Pinch of Salt
- 6 Tbsp Whole Milk

Directions

Grease grab a tube/ring cake tin. Because this is a cake, it might be a good plan to do a bit of air fryer preheating (350° F).

Grab a bowl & cream the butter & sugar together until, well, creamy? Then add the egg & mix until fluffy. Sift in the flour & salt, then mix in the milk. Keep the mixing light. Pour the batter into the cake ring & pop into the fryer.

Cook at 350° F for 15 min. Poke the cake with a toothpick & if it comes out clean, you are done. Turn the cake out & leave to cool for around 20 min.

Dust with a bit of icing (confectioners) sugar.

Rosemary Chips

Some tasty fries with salt & rosemary!

Serves: 2
Time to Prepare: 40 min

Ingredients

- 2 Potatoes
- ½ Tbsp Olive Oil
- 1 Tsp Freshly Minced Rosemary
- A Pinch or So of Salt
- 1 Small Container of Store-bought Dip (Or make your own)

Directions

Fill a large bowl with clean water. Set aside.

Clean & slice the potatoes once vertically. To make chips, you will have to slice them very finely. You can use a knife, a potato peeler (recommended), or a high-speed grater that has a slicer disk. Or the slicer slit on the good old fashioned grater. As you go, pop the slices into the water bowl. Leave them to soak for 10 min & throw the water out. Repeat this 3 times.

If your fryer needs preheating, dial it to 350° F so long. Pat the potatoes dry with a clean cloth or kitchen paper & toss them with olive oil, then toss them into the fryer basket. Cook until golden (30 min), tossing them around every so often to ensure even cooking.

When the potatoes are done, turn them out the basket into a bowl & toss with rosemary & salt. Serve with dip & enjoy!

Tip: If the dip seems to hard & thick, stir it with a little sour cream or mayonnaise & it will be easier to handle.

Classic Grilled Cheese for Two (or One)

This is just the basic temperature & timing guide for any toasted cheese sammie, really

Serves: 2
Time to Prepare: 10 min

Ingredients

- 4 Slices of Bread
- ½ cup Cheese
- ½ cup Melted Butter

Directions

Brush the melted butter over the 4 slices of bread. Scatter cheese on two of the pieces & close.

Pre-heat the fryer (if needed) to 355° F & fry until the cheese has melted & the bread is golden (4–5 min).

Parmesan Schnitzel for One

Because single people also need to eat… You could substitute the parmesan for another hard cheese if you prefer

Serves: 1
Time to Prepare: 10 min

Ingredients

- 1 Crumbed Schnitzel (Your meat of choice)
- ¼ cup Grated Parmesan
- 3 Tbsp Pasta Sauce (Reasonably Thick)

Directions

Cook the schnitzel for 15 min at 350° F for around 15 min. You could eat it at this point, but that would be boring.

Blob as much sauce on as you like & cover with cheese (generously). Pop it back into the fryer until the meat is cooked to your liking & the cheese is just perfect.

Serve with a fresh salad to be healthy & all that.

Roast Lamb Chops

Simple & convenient. Lick your chops while waiting, eat them when they are roasted.

Serves: 4
Time to Prepare: 15 min

Ingredients

- 8 Little Lamb Chops (2 chops per person)
- 1 Large Bulb of Garlic
- 3 Tbsp Vegetable Oil
- 1 Tbsp Freshly Chopped Oregano
- Sea or Koshering Salt
- Freshly Ground Pepper
- Garlic Sauce, for Serving

Directions

Get your fryer heating to 400° F. Coat the bulb of garlic with a bit of oil & pop it in the fryer for 12 min to roast. Set aside when done.

Mix the salt, herbs, & seasoning with the oil. Coat each chop with ±½ Tbsp of this herbed oil. Set aside for at least 5 min.

When the chops have had their oil pampering, pop four of them into the fryer (400° F) for 5–8 min, depending on the thickness of the chops & how well you want them done.

Pink in the middle is perfectly acceptable. Keep them warm while you cook the other four.

Now, find the bulb of garlic & neatly slice the lid off. Squeeze the cloves between your fingers to release some "juice" into the remaining herb oil. Season to taste & stir well.

Serve with the garlic oil.

Ba-corn Crustless Quiche

Bacon, corn, bell pepper, celery & onion in a beautifully smooth, rich, savory egg custard. With cheese, naturally.

Serves: 6
Time to Prepare: 10 min

Ingredients

- 1 Tbsp Butter
- 4 Strips Bacon, Roughly Chopped
- 1½–2 cups Corn Kernels
- 1 Small Yellow Onion, Finely Chopped (¾ cup)
- 1 Small Red Bell Pepper, Finely Chopped (½ cup)
- 1 Large Stalk Celery, Finely Chopped (¼ cup)
- 2 Tsp Garlic
- 1 Tsp Fresh Thyme Leaves
- 1½ cups Full Cream Milk
- ½ cup Heavy Cream
- 4 Medium Eggs
- ½ Tsp Table Salt
- ¼ Tsp Ground Cayenne Pepper
- 3–4 Slices of Old Bread, Cubed (3 cups)
- 1 cup Grated Monterey Jack Cheese (4 oz)
- 3 Tbsp Finely Grated Parmesan

Directions

Start by greasing a deep casserole dish with butter. Set aside for later.

Fry up the bacon until crispy, keep the fat in the pan once the bacon is out & use it to fry up the corn. Stir often until the corn is lightly browned & soft (10 min).

Now add the chopped up celery, onion, & red pepper & cook for a further 5 minutes. Finally, add the garlic & thyme, give it a stir & take the pan off the heat.

Grab a large bowl & whisk together the milk, cream, & eggs. Add in the fried ingredients. Season well with salt & Cayenne pepper & then fold in the bread & Jack cheese. The bread should absorb quite a bit of the moisture.

Pour into the prepared casserole dish, pop into the fryer & cook for 30 min at 320° F. Once done, scatter the parmesan cheese over the top & cook for a further 30 min.

Allow to cool for 20 min before serving.

Chimichurri Skirt Steak

An Argentinian marinade that has a lovely piquant flavor. The steak is just called "skirt". No pop star musicians' outfits are involved.

Serves: 2
Time to Prepare: 15 min

Ingredients

- 2 x 8 oz Skirt Steak
- 1 cup Finely Chopped Parsley
- ¼ cup Finely Chopped Mint
- 2 Tbsp Fresh Oregano (Washed & finely chopped)
- 3 Finely Chopped Cloves of Garlic
- 1 Tsp Red Pepper Flakes (Crushed)
- 1 Tbsp Ground Cumin
- 1 Tsp Cayenne Pepper
- 2 Tsp Smoked Paprika
- 1 Tsp Salt
- ¼ Tsp Pepper
- ¾ cup Oil
- 3 Tbsp Red Wine Vinegar

Directions

Throw all the ingredients in a bowl (besides the steak) & mix well. Put ¼ cup of the mixture in a plastic baggie with the steak & leave in the fridge overnight (2–24hrs).

Leave the bag out at room temperature for at least 30 min before popping into the fryer. Preheat for a minute or two to 390° F before cooking until med-rare (8–10 min).

Put 2 Tbsp of the chimichurri mix on top of each steak before serving.

Buttermilk Biscuits

Quick & tasty! Only takes a few minutes to bake these beauties. Enjoy with butter & honey or your favorite preserves. Best made in the food processor, see directions #2 below

Serves: 1–10
Time to Prepare: 15 min

Ingredients

- 1¼ cups All-purpose Flour
- ½ cup Cake Flour
- ½ Tsp Baking Powder
- ¼ Tsp Baking Soda
- 1 Tsp Fine Sugar
- ¾ Tsp Salt
- 4 Tbsp (Cold) Butter in Little Cubes
- ¾ cup Buttermilk
- 1 Tbsp Melted Butter for Brushing

Directions #1

Sift together the dry ingredients (flours, raising agents, sugar, & salt). Add the butter cubes & work it in with your hands. Stop when the bits of butter are quite small, but still visible. Now pour in the buttermilk & stir until dough forms. Stop immediately; the more you mix & handle the dough, the tougher the biscuits will become.

Press the dough out lightly onto a floured work surface, to about ½" thick. Use a 1¾" cutter & cut out 10 rounds. Arrange in a pie dish & brush with melted butter.

Cook at 400° F until golden (8 min). Enjoy the soft, fluffy wonders with absolutely anything.

Directions #2

Add all the dry ingredients to the processor pot. Give it a whirl for 30 sec or so to aerate & mix the ingredients.

Then add the butter cubes & run the machine again for about 30 seconds or so.

Lastly, add the buttermilk & very gently pulse until just combined. Continue as above.

Air Fried Pecan Pie

A classic winner. Super easy recipe for a delicious treat for afternoon tea.

Serves: 2
Time to Prepare: 25 min

Ingredients

- 1 x 9" Rolled out Pie Dough, Room Temp
- 1 Tbsp Butter
- ½ cup Roughly Chopped Pecan Nuts
- ¼ cup Pecan Nut Halves
- 3 Medium Eggs
- ¾ cup Maple Syrup
- 2 Tbsp Brown Sugar
- 2 Tbsp Smooth Nut Butter of Choice (e.g. Almond, cashew or peanut)
- ¾ Tsp Vanilla
- ½ Tsp Salt
- ½ Tsp Cinnamon
- A Generous Pinch of Nutmeg (⅛ Tsp)

Directions

Lay the dough out on a lightly dusted work surface. Use an 8" plate as a template to cut out the right size.

Spray the pie dish with cooking spray & lay the circle of dough inside. Tuck the edges back under themselves to form a rim & press them down with a fork. Cover & set aside.

Sauté the ½ cup of chopped nuts in butter over a medium heat until the nuts are slightly toasted & the butter is no longer foaming. Spread evenly in the pie shell.

Whisk together the eggs, syrup, sugar, nut butter, vanilla essence/extract, salt, cinnamon, & nutmeg. Pour over the toasted nuts. Use the remaining ¼ cup of nuts to make the top look pretty. Cook at 320° F for 25 min.

Leave to cool for 20 min before removing from the pie pan. You can serve this with cream or ice-cream if you like.

Stuffed Pumpkin

Butternut is an excellent veg for stuffing (not for pillows & pockets). Pick one with a large seed bulb so there is lots of room for the stuffing. If you are having trouble with overly-hard pumpkin, it may be a good idea to pre-cook it with a little oil brushed over it.

Serves: 6
Time to Prepare: 15 min

Ingredients

- ½ Butternut or Pumpkin
- 1 Med Onion, Finely Minced
- 1 Carrot, Finely Diced
- 1 Parsnip, Finely Diced
- 1 Sweet Potato, Finely Diced
- 2 Cloves Garlic, Finely Minced
- 2 Tsp Herb Mix
- 1 Egg

Directions

Scrape the seeds out. Mix the other ingredients together in a bowl (onion, carrot, parsnip, sweet potato, garlic, peas, herbs, & egg). Now pop this into the cavity.

Preheat if needed & cook at 350° F for at least half an hour.

Stuffed Potatoes

Twice fried: a yummy concoction involving potato, bacon bits, & cheese in a potato skin shell. Idaho or russet potatoes make an excellent choice here.

Serves: 2
Time to Prepare: 15 min

Ingredients

- 1 x ±15 oz Potato
- 1 Tsp Olive Oil
- 2 Bacon Strips Roughly Chopped
- ⅓ cup Grated Cheddar
- 1 Tbsp Finely Sliced Scallion/Green Onion
- 2 Tbsp Heavy Cream
- 1 Tbsp Butter
- ¼ Tsp Salt
- A Generous Pinch of Pepper (⅛ Tsp)

Directions

Coat the potato in oil & put into the basket of the fryer. Set the temp to 400° F for 60 min. The potato should be tender, but not falling apart. Remove it & leave to cool for at least 20 min.

In the meantime, sauté the bacon over a medium heat until golden & perfectly crispy (10 min). Keep the fat! Set aside (out of reach).

Slice the potato in half lengthways & scoop out the inside with a teaspoon – leaving a ¼" border next to the skin. Now mix the scooped out potato with the bacon bits & fat, ¼ cup cheese, 1½ Tsp green onions, cream, butter, salt, & pepper. Whisk until smooth.

Divide this mix between the two shells & top with the remaining cheese. Pop them back into the basket, side-by-side. Cook at 400° F until the cheese has melted & the top looks golden (20 min)

Serve hot & garnish with the remaining green scallion/onion slices.

Cajun Shrimp with Jambalaya Rice

Shrimps & prawns are pretty much interchangeable terms, depending on the country you are in. Either way, pick some biggish fellas & get cookin'!

Serves: 4
Time to Prepare: 15 min

Ingredients

- 16–20 Tiger Prawns (±1 lb)
- ½ Tsp Cayenne Pepper
- 1 Tsp Old Bay Seasoning
- ½ Tsp Paprika (Half plain, half smoked)
- ¼ Tsp Salt
- 3 Tbsp Oil

Jambalaya Rice:

- 1 Small Finely Diced Red Onion (½ cup)
- 1 Large Stalk Celery, Minced (½ cup)
- ½ cup Minced Jalapeños
- 2 Large Tomatoes, Finely Diced (1 cup)
- ¼ Tsp Cayenne Pepper
- ½ Tsp Paprika (Half regular, half smoked)
- ¼ Tsp Old Bay Spice
- 1¼ cup Chicken Broth/stock
- 1 cup Rice (Long-grain rice preferably)
- 1 Tbsp Oil
- ½ Tsp Salt

Directions

Grab a small bowl & mix all the shrimp ingredients together (oil, salt, & seasoning with the prawns). Set aside.

Now make the rice. Fry the onions, celery, chilies over a med heat, covered. Stir every so often until the onion is translucent (±5 min).

Then pour in the rice, stir to coat & then pour in the stock. Bring to the boil & then cook on low until the liquid has been absorbed (15 min).

Get the air fryer going at 390° F & cook the prawns for 5 min; then serve atop the rice.

Air Fried Broccoli

Could broccoli ever be interesting? Indeed, it could. No more childhood scars & phobias here. Open your mouth & close your eyes & you shall get a big surprise. You can thank your mama later

Serves: 2
Time to Prepare: 10 min

Ingredients

- 2 lb Bite-sized Broccoli Florets
- 2 Tbsp Olive Oil
- 1 Tsp Kosher Salt (½ Tsp table salt)
- ½ Tsp Black Pepper
- ⅓ cup Kalamata Olives (Halved)
- 2 Tsp Fresh Lemon Zest
- ¼ cup Parmesan Shavings

Directions

Blanche the florets in boiling water for 4 minutes, drain well & toss with oil & seasoning.

Pop into the fryer basket & cook at 400° F for 15 min. Give it a stir half way to ensure even cooking.

Now pop the cooked broccoli into a bowl with olives, lemon zest, & cheese. Serve immediately!

Chicken Fillets, Brie & Ham

Little roasted parcels that will never fail to impress. Serve with mashed potatoes & seasonal vegetables.

Serves: 4
Time to Prepare: 15 min

Ingredients

- 2 Large Chicken Fillets
- Freshly Ground Black Pepper
- 4 Small Slices of Brie (Or your cheese of choice)
- 1 Tbsp Freshly Chopped Chives
- 4 Slices Cured Ham

Directions

Slice the fillets into four & make incisions as you would for a hamburger bun. Leave a little "hinge" uncut at the back. Season the inside & pop some brie & chives in there. Close them & wrap them each in a slice of ham. Brush with oil & pop them into the basket.

Heat your fryer to 350° F & roast the little parcels until they look tasty (15 min)

Beef & Lemon Schnitzel for One

A simple meal that can be beautifully paired with an oaked red or medium-dry white wine

Serves: 1
Time to Prepare: 10 min

Ingredients

- 2 Tbsp Oil
- 2-3 oz Breadcrumbs
- 1 Whisked Egg in a Saucer/Soup Plate
- 1 Beef Schnitzel
- 1 Freshly Picked Lemon

Directions

Mix the oil & breadcrumbs together until loose & crumbly. Dip the meat into the egg & then into the crumbs. Make sure that it is evenly covered.

Gently place in the fryer basket & cook at 350° F (preheat if needed) until done. The timing will depend on the thickness of the schnitzel, but for a relatively thin one, it should take roughly 12 min.

Serve with a lemon half & a garden salad.

Donuts & Cinnamon

On every fryer's bucket list.... be it a deep fryer or an air fryer!

Serves: 8
Time to Prepare: 15 min

Ingredients

- 2 Tbsp Butter, Room Temperature
- ½ cup Table Sugar
- 2 ¼ cup White Cake Flour
- 1 ½ Tsp Baking Powder (Not soda)
- 1 Tsp Salt
- 2 Large Egg Yolks
- ½ cup Sour Cream
- 2 oz Melted Butter

Cinnamon Sugar:

- ⅓ cup Finely Granulated (Caster) Sugar with 1 Tsp Cinnamon

Directions

If you have a food processor or mixer, pop the butter & sugar in together & mix until it is loose again. Then stir in the yolks.

Now for the dry ingredients. In a separate bowl, sift the flour, baking powder, & salt together.

Get your butter–sugar & add in there ½ of the flour mix & ½ the sour cream. Mix well & then repeat with the remaining flour & cream. Set aside (the fridge is a recommended spot).

Lightly flour your work surface & roll the dough out to a little less than ½" thick. Use a cup/jar/cookie cutter to make the larger circles & a bottle lid to press out the smaller circle if you don't have a dedicated tool for this.

Get the air fryer to 350° F. Now brush the melted butter onto both sides of the doughnuts before popping them in for around 8 min. As soon as they come out, paint them again & coat with cinnamon sugar.

Tasty Tenders

If you don't happen to have these on hand, you can rustle sub with chicken breasts (cut into strips). Some chicken breasts even come with the tenders still attached. Crumbed tenders done this way are perfect for younger folk & make great lunchbox snacks

Serves: 4
Time to Prepare: 15 min

Ingredients

- 1lb Chicken Tenders
- 3 Whole Eggs, Whisked
- 1 cup Flour
- 1 cup Breadcrumbs (Flavor to your discretion)
- ¼ cup Vegetable Oil
- 1 Tsp Table Salt & 1½ Tsp Black Pepper (If needed)

Directions

- Plate #1: The egg

- Plate #2: The flour

- Plate #3: Oil mixed with breadcrumbs. If you are using plain or home-made crumbs, mix in the salt & pepper.

If you like, you can set your fryer so long to 320° F.

Roll the tenders in the flour, shake off excess. Then into the egg & lastly into the oil-crumb mix. Press the crumbs in to make sure they stick. Pop on a plate & set aside until all the meat is coated.

Put roughly half the tenders in the basket at a time to avoid over-crowding. Cook for 5 min, shake the basket up & cook for another 5-7 min.

Korean Chicken Satay

According to Wiki, satay is an Indonesian/Malaysian dish of meat on a stick with a spicy sauce. So this is classified as fusion food.

Serves: 4
Time to Prepare: 15 min

Ingredients

- 1 lb Chicken Tenders, Trimmed of Excess Fat
- ½ cup Soy Sauce of Choice
- ½ cup Pineapple Juice
- ¼ cup Light Sesame Oil
- 4 Cloves of Garlic, Minced
- 4 Sliced Green Onions
- 1 Smallish Ginger Root, Grated (1 Tbsp)
- 2 Tsp Toasted Sesame Seeds
- A Pinch of Freshly Ground Black Pepper

Directions

Skewer the chicken & then mix all the other ingredients in a bowl. Put the skewers into the marinade & leave in the fridge overnight, if possible (2–24hrs).

When you are ready, set (if needed, preheat) the fryer to 390° F, & cook the skewers in two batches; ±6 min each batch.

Steamed Salmon & Sauce

Steaming in your fryer is entirely possible & makes the most wonderfully tender fish

Serves: 2
Time to Prepare: 15 min

Ingredients

- 1 cup Water
- 2 x 6 oz Fresh Salmon
- 2 Tsp Vegetable Oil
- A Pinch of Salt for Each Fish
- ½ cup Plain Greek Yogurt
- ½ cup Sour Cream
- 2 Tbsp Finely Chopped Dill (Keep a bit for garnishing)
- A Pinch of Salt to Taste

Directions

Pour the water into the bottom of the fryer & start heating to 285° F.

Drizzle oil over the fish & spread it. Salt the fish to taste. Now pop it into the fryer for ±10 min.

In the meantime, mix the yogurt, cream, dill & a bit of salt to make the sauce. When the fish is done, serve with the sauce & garnish with sprigs of dill.

Onion Flowers

The most beautiful & unusual thing to try. Definitely a center-piece, for sure. "I'm a lonely little petunia in an onion patch..."

Serves: 4
Time to Prepare: 10 min +

Ingredients

- 4 Med-sized Onions
- 1 Tbsp Olive Oil
- 4 Tsp Soft Butter

Directions

Cut off the top & bottom of the onions as close to the edge as possible. Carefully remove the outer shell layer. Let it stand on one of the cut sides, then slice 4–8 times vertically – not all the way through, but almost.

You need a little bit of flesh at the bottom to anchor the "petals". Your onion will now resemble a closed flower bud, & if viewed from above, a pizza.

Pop the onions into some salty water & leave them to soak there for about 4 hours. This helps the "petals" to open & takes the sharp flavor down a good couple of notches.

When they are ready, heat your fryer to 350° F (if you need to pre-heat it). Place the onion "blossoms" in the basket, drip a bit of oil over them & drop a blob of butter in the center of each one. Cook for 30 min.

Tip: Remove the outer layer if it looks unappetizing

Pork & Peanut Satay

Enjoy the bits of meat without the stick part...

Serves: 4
Time to Prepare: 35 min

Ingredients

- 2 Crushed Cloves of Garlic
- ±1" Finger of Ginger Root, Grated (Or 1 Tsp ground, dried ginger)
- 2 Tsp Hot Pepper Sauce
- 2½ Tbsp Sweet Soy Sauce
- 2 Tbsp Oil
- 14oz Cubed Pork (1" cubes)
- 1 Finely Sliced Shallot
- 1 Tsp Ground Coriander Seeds
- 1 cup Coconut Milk (Canned)
- ±3½ oz Unsalted Peanuts, Ground Fairly Finely

Directions

Make the marinade:

- Grab a dish & mix the ginger, hot sauce, half the garlic, 1 Tbsp oil & 1 Tbsp soy sauce. Combine this mixture with the pork & leave to sit for at least 15 min or so.

Set your fryer to 400° F & pop the meat into the basket. Roast until brown, turn after 6 min to ensure even cooking & then roast for a final 6 min.

While all that excitement is happening in the fryer, mix up the peanut sauce:

- Heat a little pot over a medium heat & sauté the shallot & remaining garlic. When the onion starts to become soft &

translucent, add in the coriander & fry gently until fragrant. Now mix in the peanut powder, coconut milk, 1 Tsp hot sauce & 1 Tbsp soy sauce. Bring to the boil & leave to simmer, stirring regularly for 5 min. If the sauce thickens a wee bit too much, add a touch of water. Season to taste.

Serve the cubes over rice with the sauce.

Tossed Vegetable Medley

Air fried zucchini, yellow squash, & carrots. If you have toddlers or small children, this is an excellent way to get them to eat veggies. Even adults need a little fun on their plates now & then

Serves: 2
Time to Prepare: 10 min

Ingredients

- ½ lb Carrot Cubes (± 1")
- 6 Tsp Olive Oil
- 1 lb Zucchini "Middles" Sliced Lengthways (Chopped into ¾")
- 1 lb Yellow Squash, Prepared Same As Zucchini
- 1 Tsp Kosher Salt (½ Tsp table salt)
- ½ Tsp White Pepper (Has a much lighter flavor than black)
- 1 Tbsp Ripped Up Tarragon Leaves

Directions

Toss (#1) the carrot cubes in 2 Tsp of oil & pop into the fryer basket at 400° F for 5 min.

In the meantime, season the zucchini & squash bits & toss (#2) in the remaining 4 Tsp oil. Add this to the carrots when they are done. Keep the temp at 400° F & cook for 30 min. If your machine does not have paddles to stir it for you, remove the basket once or twice during cooking & give it a good toss (#3) to ensure even browning.

The final toss (#4), will be with the tarragon leaves (or suitable sub) once the veggies are all cooked. Serve warm.

Stuffed Peppers

This recipe can quite easily be turned vegan-friendly if the cheese & bread are swapped out for suitable alternatives

Serves: 6
Time to Prepare: 15 min

Ingredients

- 6 Bell Peppers
- 1 Carrot, Finely Diced
- 1 Small Onion, Finely Diced
- 1 Potato, Finely Diced
- 1 Bread Roll, Finely Diced
- 2 Cloves Garlic, Finely Minced
- ½ cup Peas
- 2 Tsp Herb Mix
- ⅓ Shredded Cheese of Choice

Directions

Cut the lids off the peppers (don't throw them out just yet) & clean the insides of each pepper up.

Salvage any flesh from the lids & chop it up finely, then mix with the carrot, potato, bread, & garlic. Add the peas & herbs & mix well.

If your fryer needs preheating, get it going at 350° F so long. Stuff the peppers, but leave the cheese off for now. Cook for 20 min.

Now add the cheese & cook for another 5 min.

YUM!

Radish & Mozzarella Salad

A brilliantly simple & elegant answer to a boring salad. Play with the shape of the cheese; cut into wedges, sticks, half-moons or squares & arrange on a platter with the fried radishes.

Serves: 4
Time to Prepare: 5 min

Ingredients

- 1¼ lb Fresh Radishes (Can leave the tops on if you like)
- 2 Tbsp Vegetable Oil
- 1 Tsp Salt
- ½ Tsp Black Pepper
- ½ lb Fresh Mozzarella Sliced into ½" Bits
- 2 Tbsp Balsamic Glaze
- Extra-virgin Olive Oil for Serving

Directions

Clean the radishes thoroughly (make sure there is no sand under the tops). Dry with kitchen paper & trim away anything that does not look appetizing (dead leaves etc.).

Toss them well with oil, salt, & pepper & pop into the basket of the fryer. Cook at 350° F for 30 min. Toss them around once or twice to ensure even cooking (unless your model has a paddle).

Arrange the cooked radishes on a serving plate with the cheese. Drizzle with the olive oil & balsamic glaze.

Marinated Cornish Hen

Feel like something a little fancier than the same old roast chicken? This meat is similar in flavor – being a hen & all – but is much more tender & succulent

Serves: 4
Time to Prepare: 15 min

Ingredients

- 1 Cornish Bird (±2 lb)
- ½ cup Vegetable Oil of Choice
- ¼ Tsp Red Pepper Flakes
- 1 Tsp Freshly Chopped Thyme
- 1 Tsp Freshly Chopped Rosemary
- ¼ Tsp Salt
- ¼ Tsp Sugar
- 1 Lemon, Zested

Directions

Mix all the ingredients in a large bowl (except the hen). Set aside.

Grab a good sharp, chef's knife & look professional. Pop the hen on the cutting board with the legs in & its belly facing away from you. Remove the backbone: make two cuts from the top to the bottom. Now split the hen lengthways (you will have to cut through the breastbone).

Introduce the marinade to the hen & leave them to become acquainted overnight (1–24hrs).

When you are ready to cook, strain the hen to get any excess liquid off & get the fryer to 390° F. Cook until the leg has an internal temp of 165° F (±15 min).

Air Fried Banana Bread

A beautifully soft classic. Serve warm with whipped, sweetened cream

Serves: 1 loaf
Time to Prepare: 15 min

Ingredients

- 4 Tbsp Soft Butter
- 2 Tsp Soft Butter
- ¾ cup Flour, Plus More for Dusting the Pan
- ½ Banana (Overripe)
- ¼ cup Brown Sugar
- 3 Med Eggs
- ¼ cup Fine Sugar
- ¾ Tsp Vanilla Essence
- 1 Tsp Cinnamon
- ¼ Tsp Nutmeg
- ¼ Tsp Salt
- ¼ Tsp Bicarbonate of Soda (Baking soda)
- ⅛ Tsp Baking Powder
- ⅓ cup Chopped Pecan Nuts

Directions

Grease a loaf pan (roughly 6x3x2" pan) with 2 Tsp of butter. Sprinkle a little flour inside & turn the pan so that all the sides are lightly dusted. Keep one side for the batter.

Mash half the banana with the sugar, then add the eggs, sugar, vanilla, cinnamon, nutmeg, & salt. Whisk together a little, just to mix. Sift the baking soda, baking powder & flour into the bowl & stir in. Then add the nutty bits.

Scoop into the baking pan & pop it into the fryer. Set to 320° F for 50 minutes. Test for doneness with a wooden skewer or a clean butter knife: it should come out clean.

Lift the pan out of the basket using tongs & leave to cool for at least 20 min.

Slip a spatula around the sides to make sure it is nice & loose & then invert it onto a plate. Slice & serve warm.

Cheesy Garlic Bread

A classic necessity in every home! Homemade garlic seasoning is hard to beat, so here is a quick guide to what you can stir together instead

Serves: 2
Time to Prepare: 10 min

Ingredients

- 2 Dinner Rolls
- ½ cup Grated Cheese (Your choice!)
- 2 Tbsp Melted Butter
- Garlic Bread Seasoning Mix

Directions

Cut the bread at regular intervals, as far down as possible without actually cutting off slices. Be creative here! Bury the grated cheese in the slits, paint the top of the rolls with butter & sprinkle seasoning on top.

Preheat your fryer if need be & cook at 350° F until the cheese has melted (5 min).

Homemade Garlic Seasoning:

Combine the following ingredients in a sealable jar. It can stay fresh for at least a month in the fridge:

- ¼ cup Powdered Parmesan
- ¼ Tsp Salt
- 1 Tbsp Garlic Powder
- 1 Tsp Oregano (Dried)
- 1 Tsp Basil (Dried)
- 1 Tsp Parsley (Dried)

Flying Fish

If chips can be fried in thin air, why not the fish too?

Serves: 6
Time to Prepare: 10 min

Ingredients

- 4 Tbsp Oil
- 3–4 oz Breadcrumbs
- 1 Whisked Whole Egg in a Saucer/Soup Plate
- 4 Fresh Fish Fillets
- Fresh Lemon (For serving)

Directions

Preheat the fryer (if necessary) to 350° F. Mix the crumbs & oil until it looks nice & loose.

Dip the fish in the egg & coat lightly, then move on to the crumbs. Make sure the fillet is covered evenly.

Cook in the air fryer basket for roughly 12 minutes – depending on the size of the fillets you are using.

Serve with fresh lemon & chips to complete the duo.

French Air Fried Beans

A delicious & simple dish of French green beans, shallots & slivered almonds

Serves: 4
Time to Prepare: 5 min

Ingredients

- 1½ lb Green Beans, Cleaned Up
- 1 Tbsp Salt
- 1 Tsp Salt
- ½ lb Shallots, Quartered
- ½ Tsp White Pepper
- 2 Tbsp Olive Oil
- ¼ cup Toasted, Slivered Almonds

Directions

Blanch the beans in boiling, salted (1 Tbsp) water for 2 minutes. Drain well.

Pop the beans into a large bowl with 1 Tsp of salt, white pepper, oil, & shallots. Toss to combine & coat evenly. Cook in the fryer basket at 400° F until lightly browned & tender (25 min). Stir once or twice during the cooking process.

Serve hot. Enjoy!

Shirred Eggs

There is absolutely no alcohol in this recipe. Shirred eggs are kind of like Eggs Benedict & are served any time of day in the dish they were cooked.

Serves: 2
Time to Prepare: 5 min

Ingredients

- 2 Tsp Butter
- 2 Thin Slices of Ham
- 4 Large Eggs
- 2 Tbsp Heavy Cream
- ¾ Tsp Kosher Salt (Half the amount for regular table salt)
- ¼ Tsp Black Pepper
- 3 Tbsp Finely Grated Parmesan Cheese
- A Generous Pinch of Smoked Paprika (⅛ Tsp)
- 2 Tsp Freshly Chopped Chives

Directions

Grab a pie pan & butter it up. Then lay the ham slices down so the bottom & sides of the pan are covered completely. Cover & set aside.

Now take one of the eggs & whisk it (after cracking it open, obviously) with the cream, ¼ Tsp of the salt & a generous pinch of black pepper.

Pour this mixture into the ham–pan, then crack the remaining eggs over the top of this. Be careful not to break the yolks. Season well & sprinkle with cheese. Bake at 320° F for 12 minutes.

Once done, scatter the bits of chives & smoked paprika over the top. Carefully remove the eggs from the pan with a spatula & slip them onto a plate.

Simple Spring Rolls

Acquire a packet of spring rolls from an Asian market near the noodles or make your own if you have the time. This filling is delicious even on its own!

Serves: 10
Time to Prepare: 20 mins

Ingredients

- 1.75 oz Bean Thread Noodles (Glass/Cellophane Noodles)
- 1 Tbsp Sesame Oil
- 7 oz Mince
- 1 Small Diced Onion
- 3 Crushed Cloves of Garlic
- 1 cup Mixed Vegetables
- 1 Tsp Soy Sauce
- 10 Spring Roll Skins
- 2 Tbsp Cold Water

Directions

Soak the noodles in some hot water to make them easier to work with. Drain & trim them into manageable lengths.

Grab a wok & fry the onion, garlic, mince & mixed veg until the mince is more-or-less browned. You are now done with the cooking part of prep.

Throw in the soy sauce & give it a stir, followed by the noodles. Leave the ingredients for a while to become acquainted. Once the juices have been absorbed you are ready to begin assembly.

Lay out one spring roll sheet. Lay a strip of filling across it (diagonally), then fold the top corner down over the filling. Bring the two sides across & then roll it up. Kind of like an envelope gone wrong. Daub a little water on the last bit of the roll to help it seal. Repeat this exercise until you have all 10 done.

Brush each roll with oil & pop into your air fryer for 8 min at 350° F. You may need to cook them in batches or layers to get them all perfect.

Baked Tomato & Feta

Bunless & brilliant. An interesting take on a caprice salad, really.

Serves: 2
Time to Prepare: 20 min

Ingredients

Toasted Pine Nuts:

- 3 Tbsp Pine Nuts & 1 Tsp Olive Oil

Basil Pesto:

- 1 Bunch Roughly Chopped Fresh Parsley (½ cup)
- 1 Bunch Roughly Chopped Fresh Basil (½ cup)
- ½ cup Shredded Parmesan
- 3 Tbsp Pine Nuts
- ½ cup Olive Oil
- 1 Clove of Garlic
- Pinch of Salt – to Taste

The Rest of the Ingredients:

- 1 Tomato, Thickly Sliced (½" Slices)
- 1 x Block of Feta (±8 oz), Also Sliced (½" Slices)
- 1 Small Onion Thinly Sliced (½ cup), Tossed in 1 Tbsp Olive Oil

Directions

Toast the pine nuts:

- Mix the pine nuts with 1 Tsp oil & salt & pop into the air fryer basket for a minute or two on 390° F. If you like, you can preheat the oven a little to reduce cooking time. Toss them around a bit to make sure they are evenly cooked. Leave to cool on a kitchen towel.

Pesto:

- Pop the basil & parsley in the food processor with the cheese, garlic, toasted nuts & salt. Once the machine is running, drizzle in the olive oil. Leave in the fridge once the oil is incorporated.

Finishing the dish:

- Use a circle cutter to make nice rounds of feta to match the tomatoes. Start stacking: tomato first, then a little layer of pesto & top with a slice of onion. Carefully place each stack in the fryer & cook until the feta begins to brown & soften (12–14 min).

- Sprinkle a little salt over the top & finish off with a little pesto before serving (immediately).

Crisp Crunch Crab Cakes

These are a type of cake otherwise known as croquettes, which literally means in French, "to crunch"

Serves: 6
Time to Prepare: 30 min

Ingredients

- 1 lb Crab Meat
- 1 Small & Finely Chopped Onion (¼ cup)
- 1 Small & Finely Chopped Red Bell Pepper (¼ cup)
- 2 Tbsp Finely Minced Celery
- ¼ Tsp Freshly Minced Tarragon (Can use basil or dill instead)
- ¼ Tsp Freshly Minced Chives
- ½ Tsp Freshly Minced Parsley
- 2 Egg Whites (2–3 Tbsp)
- ¼ cup Mayonnaise
- ¼ cup Sour Cream
- ½ Tsp Ground (Dried) Cayenne Pepper
- ½ Tsp Salt
- ½ Tsp Freshly Squeezed Lime Juice
- 1 Tsp Olive Oil

Crispy Coating:

- 3 Whole Eggs, Beaten
- 1 cup Flour
- 1 cup Panko Breadcrumbs
- 1 Tsp Olive Oil
- ½ Teaspoon Salt

Directions

Over a med heat, fry the onion, pepper & celery until translucent & sweet (5 min). Set aside.

Throw all the other ingredients into a large bowl & mix heartily. Set aside.

Mix the salt & breadcrumbs & put into a soup plate or shallow dish. Likewise, put the flour in a dish & also the beaten eggs. So you now have three dishes: egg, flour, crumbs.

Preheat your fryer (if needed) to 390° F. Make shapes with the crab meat – be creative. Not everything has to be a ball. Try squares maybe. Make tangram shapes for (little) diners. Dust each shape in flour, dip in the egg & then the crumbs.

Cook the cakes in two batches at 390° F until golden; 8–10 min each batch.

Sweet Potato Chips

Make sure that you cut the chips as evenly as humanly possible. This will ensure more even cooking & will give you a more consistent result if you make this dish often.

Serves: 2
Time to Prepare: 15 min

Ingredients

- 2 Large Sweet Potatoes, Peeled & Sliced/Chopped
- A Bit of Olive Oil for Coating

Directions

Heat the fryer to 350° F (if necessary).

Coat the potato chips in some oil (roughly 2 Tbsp) & cook until tender (±15 min). If the chips are thick, you may need to add a little more time.

Tip: Put the whole lot into a bag & shake it around. Make sure the top of the bag is sealed first, though... or you may need a fresh change of clothes.

Air Fried Mac & Cheese Wheel

Super, easy & always a winner in any family. If you (or a fellow diner) has gluten issues, simple sub the noodles for gluten-free noodles & the breadcrumbs, well, for gluten-free bread crumbs

Serves: 6
Time to Prepare: 10 min

Ingredients

- 2 Tbsp Salt
- ½ Tsp Salt
- ½ lb Elbow Pasta
- ½ cup Organic Whole Milk
- ½ cup Heavy Cream
- ½ cup Shredded Fontina
- ½ cup Shredded Gruyere
- ½ cup Shredded Cheddar
- ¼ Tsp Black Pepper
- A Generous Pinch of Nutmeg
- ¼ cup White Bread Crumbs
- ¼ cup Finely Grated Parmesan
- 1 Tbsp Melted Butter

Directions

Cook the pasta with 2 Tbsp salt (as directed on the packaging), until al dente – do not overcook. Drain thoroughly & pour into the bowl you will use for the cheeses etc.

Now pour in the milk & cream, add the Fontina, Gruyere, & Cheddar, ½ Tsp salt, pepper & nutmeg. Combine well.

Find a smaller bowl & mix together: the crumbs, Parmesan, & butter. Set aside.

Assembly time! Carefully pour the pasta mix into a deep casserole dish & scatter the Parmesan mix over the top.

Place the dish in the basket of the air fryer & set the temp to 350° F for 30 min. Once done, remove the dish & leave to cool for ±20 min before serving. Turn the whole thing upside down onto a serving plate & divide it up.

Hamionshroom Quiche

An easy recipe for a ham, onion & mushroom quiche. Make your pie dough from scratch or use store-bought dough for convenience. Use an 8" pie plate.

Serves: 4
Time to Prepare: 20 min

Ingredients

- 1 x 9" Pie Dough at Room Temp
- 1 Tbsp Butter
- 2 Button Mushrooms (1 oz)
- 1 Small Yellow Onion, Diced (¼ cup)
- 2 Tbsp Little Cubes of Ham
- 2 Jumbo Eggs
- ⅓ cup Heavy Cream
- ½ Tsp Salt
- ¼ Tsp Black Pepper
- A Generous Pinch of Nutmeg (⅛ Tsp)
- ½ Tsp Chopped Thyme (If using dried, only use a pinch)
- ⅓ cup Shredded Cheese (Your choice!)

Directions

Dust your work surface with a little flour & lay the pie dough out. Grab an 8" pie dish/plate & use it as a template to cut the dough. Carefully lay the dough into the pie dish & tuck the edges back in under the dough to form a rim. Press the edges down with a fork or another object to make it pretty.

Bake blind (covered with baking parchment & beans) at 400° F for 10 min. Remove weights & paper once baked. Leave the shell to cool in the basket.

In the meantime, fry the mushrooms in the butter over a medium heat, stirring often (4–5 min). You want them well caramelized.

Now add the ham & onions & continue frying until the onions are transparent (3–4 min). Add to the pie shell.

Now whisk the eggs, cream, thyme, salt, pepper, & nutmeg together. Pour over the onion–mushroom–ham mix & scatter cheese over the top. Put the pie back into the fryer at 300° F for 40 min.

Leave to cool for at least 20 min before slicing & serving.

Vanilla Soufflé

Serve with a crème chocolate Anglaise or a fancy sauce of your choice

Serves: 4
Time to Prepare: 20 min

Ingredients

- ¼ cup White Flour
- 1 cup Full Cream Milk
- 1 Vanilla Pod
- 1 oz Sugar
- 4 Egg Yolks
- Melted Butter & Sugar (Coating inside of the ramekins)
- ¼ cup Finely Granulated Sugar
- ¼ cup Softened Butter
- 2 Tsp Vanilla Essence/Extract
- 5 Egg Whites
- 1 Tsp Cream of Tartar

Directions

Mix the flour & butter into a paste. Bring the milk, vanilla pod & sugar to the boil, then add the flour mix in & give it a good whisk to ensure there are no lumpy bits. Simmer until thick, then leave to cool for 10 min.

Coat 6 ramekins with butter & sugar. Beat the yolk & vanilla extract/essence. Put a little of the cooled mixture in with the yolk & then gradually pour this into the rest of the milk mixture.

Now beat the whites & castor sugar with the cream of tartar to medium peak stage.

Fold this into the milk & yolk mixture, being careful to keep the mix aerated. Pour into the ramekins & make the tops look pretty.

Set the fryer to 320° F & cook 3 ramekins at a time for 12–15 min. Serve with a dusting of confectioner's sugar & a drizzle of sauce.

Crispy Nachos Prawns

Here is something a little different for your next al fresco dining experience. Super easy & fun to eat.

Serves: 8
Time to Prepare: 30 min

Ingredients

- 18 Prawns (Cleaned with the nasty bits removed)
- 1 Egg, Whisked & in a Dish/Soup Plate
- 8–9 oz Nacho Flavored Chips, Crushed into Crumbs (Use a food processor)

Directions

Dip the cleaned prawns into the egg & then into the nacho crumbs.

Pop into your air fryer & cook at 350° F (preheat if needed) until they are just cooked through (8 min).

Serve them with the usual nacho toppings like salsa & guac with sour cream.

Curried Cauliflower Florets

Says who that this has to be the vegetable that wins the "bland" contest every year? Spice things up a little.

Serves: 4
Time to Prepare: 10 min

Ingredients

- ¼ cup Sultanas or Golden Raisins
- ½ cup Olive Oil
- ¼ cup Pine Nuts
- 1 Cauliflower
- 1 Tbsp Curry Powder (Spiciness up to your discretion)
- ¼ Tsp Table Salt

Directions

Soak the sultanas (or golden raisins) in a cup of boiling water.
If you need to preheat your fryer, do so now. Set it to 390° F. Toss the pine nuts with the oil & cook in the air fryer for a minute or so. Set aside.

Carefully remove the core of the cauliflower with a very sharp knife & cut the florets into bite-size chunks. Now toss the florets up with the curry powder, salt & oil.

Cook half in the fryer for 8–10 minutes & then repeat for the rest. Strain the sultanas & toss in with the pine nuts & the cauliflower.

Made in the USA
Lexington, KY
08 January 2017